Droughts

Andrea Rivera

abdopublishing.com

Published by Abdo Zoom™, PO Box 398166, Minneapolis, Minnesota 55439. Copyright © 2018 by
Abdo Consulting Group, Inc. International copyrights reserved in all countries. No part of this book may be
reproduced in any form without written permission from the publisher. Abdo Zoom™ is a trademark and logo
of Abdo Consulting Group, Inc.

Printed in the United States of America, North Mankato, Minnesota
022017
092017

Cover Photo: iStockphoto
Interior Photos: iStockphoto, 1, 10–11, 12, 13, 18–19; Eddie Hernandez Photography/iStockphoto, 4–5; Jake Osborne/
Shutterstock Images, 7; Shutterstock Images, 8; Anthony Artusa/NOAA/NWS/NCEP/CPC, 9; Dorothea Lange/FSA/
OWI Collection/Library of Congress, 14, 15; Jeffrey B. Banke/Shutterstock Images, 16–17; M. Grageda/iStockphoto,
18; Johan Larson/Shutterstock Images, 21

Editor: Brienna Rossiter
Series Designer: Madeline Berger
Art Direction: Dorothy Toth

Publisher's Cataloging-in-Publication Data
Names: Rivera, Andrea, author.
Title: Droughts / by Andrea Rivera.
Description: Minneapolis, MN : Abdo Zoom, 2018. | Series: Natural disasters |
    Includes bibliographical references and index.
Identifiers: LCCN 2017930343 | ISBN 9781532120367 (lib. bdg.) |
    ISBN 9781614797470 (ebook) | ISBN 9781614798033 (Read-to-me ebook)
Subjects: LCSH: Droughts--Juvenile literature.
Classification: DDC 363.34/929--dc23
LC record available at http://lccn.loc.gov/2017930343

Table of Contents

Science

Droughts are times with little or no rain. They are caused by **jet streams**.

Jet streams are strong winds. They move high in the sky.

Jet streams bring water from sea to land as rain. Sometimes they come at unusual times. Or they go a different way.

Then rain does not come.
A drought happens.

Technology

Scientists measure water levels.

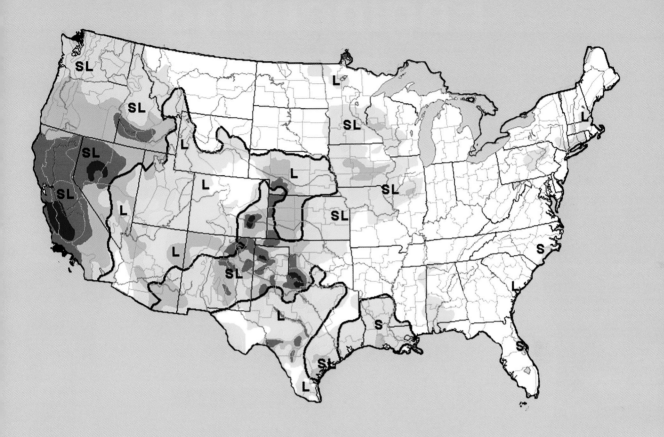

They get **data** from **satellites**, too. They use the data to make a special map. The map shows where droughts are.

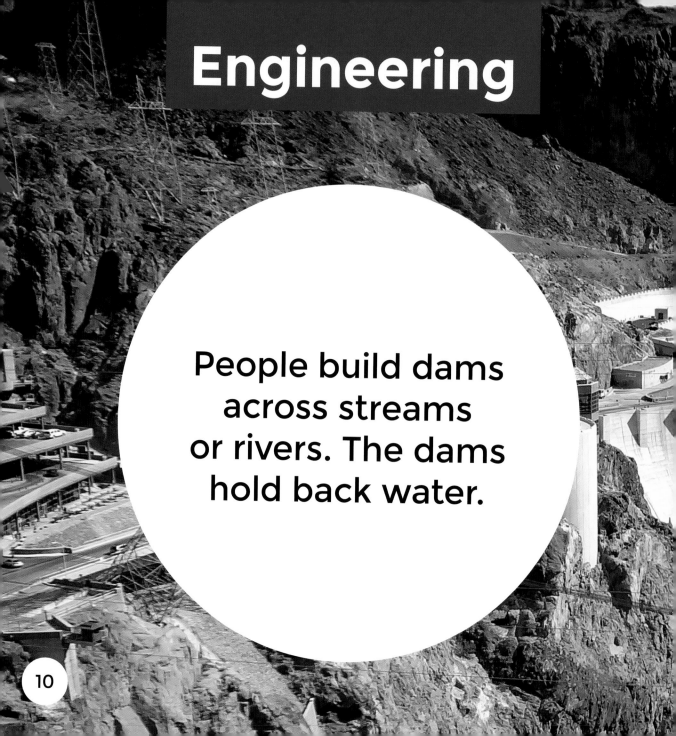

Engineering

People build dams
across streams
or rivers. The dams
hold back water.

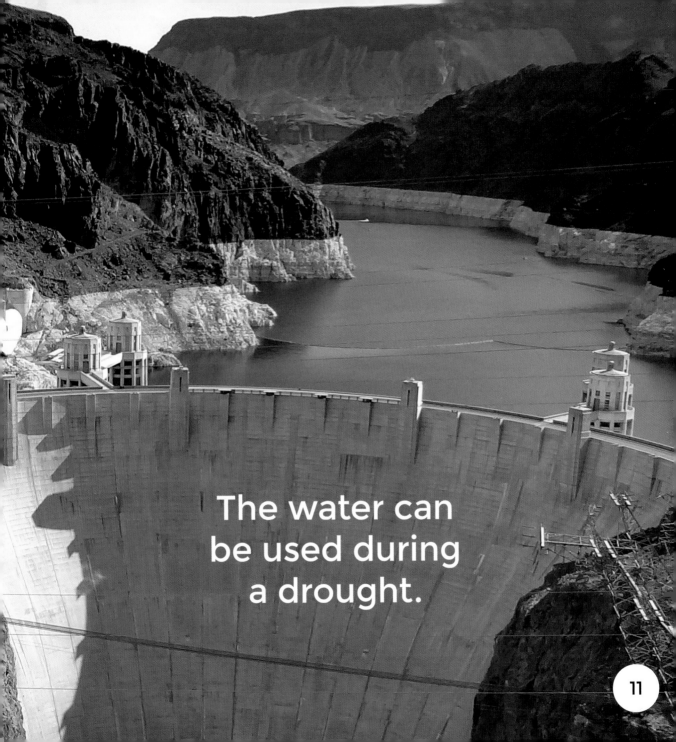

The water can
be used during
a drought.

People also pump water from aquifers.

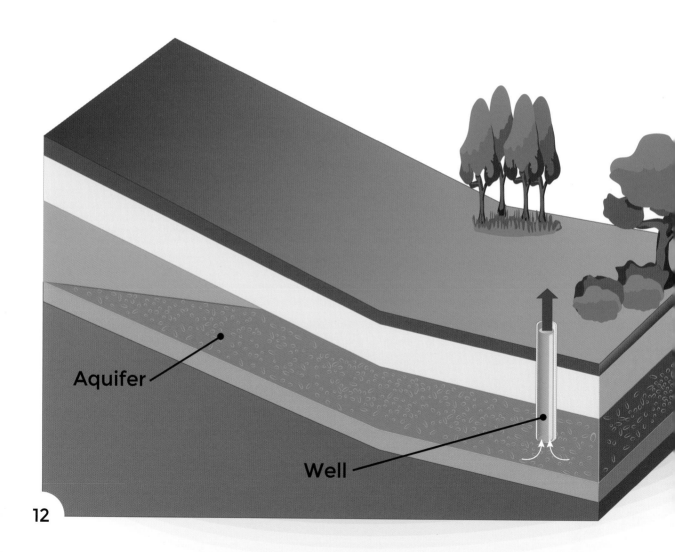

Aquifer

Well

Pipes send the water to dry places.

Art

The United States had a bad drought in the 1930s. Crops died. People became very poor.

Dorothea Lange took photos of people. Her photos told their stories.

Math

In **temperate** places a drought is 15 days in a row with less than 0.01 inches (0.25 mm) of rain.

Deserts often go weeks with no rain. They must be dry for more than 15 days to have a drought.

- Some droughts are just a few weeks long. But some can last for years or even decades.

- The drought in the 1930s affected about 65 percent of the United States.

- This drought was especially bad in the Great Plains. It affected parts of Oklahoma, Texas, Kansas, Colorado, and New Mexico.

- This area got so dry that dust blew everywhere. It was known as the Dust Bowl.

Glossary

aquifer - a layer of rock or sand that holds water.

data - information that is collected to study or plan something.

desert - a very dry, sandy area with little plant growth.

jet stream - a strong current of fast winds high above Earth's surface.

satellite - a device or object that orbits Earth.

temperate - not very hot or very cold.

Booklinks

For more information on droughts, please visit abdobooklinks.com

 In on STEAM!

Learn even more with the Abdo Zoom STEAM database. Check out abdozoom.com for more information.

Index